Tonto &
Destinata

Poems

Ted Bernal Guevara

Cover Design by Pre Miercoles

ISBN: 978-1-61704-397-0

First Edition

TABLE OF CONTENTS

ACKNOWLEDGEMENT

Vending Machine Press: "You're A Movie I Haven't Finished"

Suisun Valley Review: "Aspen Matis"

The Pangolin Review: "A Manageable War," "Full Four"

Brevis Vita: "Two Yokes"

Cathexis Northwest Press: "12 Words I Would Use in a Poem"

Sa malalayong mga puso

YOU'RE A MOVIE I HAVEN'T FINISHED

Frames of you resemble the lead in a way
that is not flimsy. The thinness of you slips under glass.

You were that saved forest I zip-lined over
I must see you in four corners

This is not on-location for me
You are in that talent de facto

You have no lines
I touch senses in the space you've occupied

My intermission does not pause you
It cuddles your face

on the wall, my breathing halts.
I shiver, shiver still, for the next scene.

                    *

How can distance have edges to fall over
or projector light that can burn
film to a stop

or placidity that tapers sleep?

7

ASPEN MATIS

Throw that cane away; let it bounce and belittle
itself among the down rocks. And please don't look

back to cradle it like Moses' staff, its blackness unworthy
of glisten, no standout among preset violets.

Yes, your onward sway can cut through fresh swirls,
your knees mincing good faith. Your youth needs

not rewind the loud clocks you may have placed
on high shelves. You look up and see only

incomplete circle on each one. If they provide
wholesome ticks, you would wish

they're only clearest, the flimsiest of water
over the next bend of pine trees. Resolved, they

are already lunged through, smashed by your
seemingly frail boots. This is what I know of you.

The stars lent faint on my sight as I try to sort
the needles and the cones. I look up

and all the luster comes from your face; my heaves
of air are not from strides the merciless

backwall may have muraled in my mind. Clusters of
violet stay motionless. Blackened canes are

just that. We breathe to see and hunger to feel

what is deeper in the soil than us. Blind me, I

just see a sprig of green from that granite; and
a growth upward webbing cracks for the air of you.

PHYSICIANS

Doctors know all the sins in the world,
the shouts and whimpers that erode their ears,
the lost sheep from one too many herds.
They've glazed their elbows and have flung
the lard away from their sight. They've sighed in
perfect births and have conjoined themselves
to brutal ones, pleading this is not the end.
They've done tricks in the streets, have dug
shortcuts to the inside even if the offshoot
is a gem to that stigma, that less state of mind.
They've adopted monotone in their voice
and proceeded. "Got you" rings

bright as usual. When their hands do peculiar,
people stare, contemplate, bemused on how
their fluids could circulate as compared to
the born odd—these protégés from assisted air.
They see too much. They go into rage, yelling,
"Leave him alone! Don't you see? He'll always
manage different!" Anger doesn't pave their paths;
and guidance falters at the side of road.
Doctors wither and die, leaving their remakes
to concoct heart valves, eye lenses, crutches
out of gravel, out of tar, gunk that hardens them.

12 WORDS I WOULD USE IN A POEM

Idle. Like a constant happening that hums
even if we submerged it
in water.

Recluse. Someone who sips from
that water and tries to see
clear the bottom.

Symphonic. Music one hears when
the thickness of the wall matches
the depth from
surface to bottom.

Burst. As in an eyeful
of the flying carp when startled.

Impetuous. A word all too poetic;
would do justice to the carp
every time.

Sensitive. What we know
of the fish. The word Impetuous
all but disagrees.

Love. What every sensible
writing teacher tells us not to use.

Drive. What they prefer instead.

Calm. What cannot be grasped after
we've just missed a pedestrian.

Breathe. What we yearn for
all the way home.

Frenzy. What quells in us
when the garage door closes.

Align. When we think of death side by side,
the engine still running. Which brings
us back to Recluse, the float side of Idle.

REZ GIRLS

Count the snow that fell on her birth.
Remote is her dig for the unseen grass.
This is her ride sliding on ice through
eras of her womanhood. She knew no other
makeup blemishing that terrain.
Give her freedom for she'd found ease
in the hardness. The miles she'd danced on now
bear tracks, for her mother under the quilt
and for her father on the backyard rock
mincing her future under that abundant sky.
Her brother has crawled back to the pad.
Count the worry dripping off his back. Count the paint
that spreads on their pop's face. All dry
with the warmth before the actual spring, a time
she would just let go with her razz flair.
Count the mountain height she saw this on
from their picture window. Count the red
in the little shadows of her footprints.
Count the number-starved, count the happy dark,
where one basks somewhere else.
Voices from a cozy bed say this place exists,
beyond momentary talk, beyond warmth
that rapines like men perpetual in the freeze.
Count the mercy that stayed behind
and cuddled up to what would be. Joy, tepid,
routine. Count the gone of women before her.
Count the graph that zigs nowhere. On the land,
it is zero—under the sky of abundance.
Count the ice, the snow, the melt that was her.

ART OF AGING

If we climb wrecked pieces of a tower
and scale them like the ants at our feet,
bold and wise beyond their years,
we have groomed ourselves to outlast
any grief. Our task is to believe beyond
the common, beyond the urge to say
what can we decipher, the disproportion
of that word, and of us, the sigh of it.
Azaleas can coerced beauty by living
beyond their directions; their fuchsia
singes into green. They keep strength but
mellow at the sight of dark; and dry.
Ants, with their tiny stamina, climb the tower.
They need no other philosophy but the gist
of busyness to laurel in their tiny years.

AT NIGHT, CROWS

Overcrowd the dark for it has many shades.
Many possibilities of where pinpoint is.
He had two children, a boy never seen
But the daughter he clasps her hand at a gun
Store, showing her not to touch the unloaded.
There was un-war in him, a place dipped in
Where red lasers zip above. His wife knew it
Too well, but what half he had left is the one
She should embrace. His other halfself was
The one putting up fences, the one bowling,
And the one grasping a loved one's hand from
Safe safety. There are beady eyes in the dark
With black broken wings, perhaps in need of
His attention, perhaps in need of what gold
They had envied of him. Crows have that
Bent of unlight. Their eyes, though starved,
Do not permit such shine. Such safe safety.

A GIRL NAMED WINTER

In the warmth of the naïve,
there's a need to seek Milano Slices.

There they are in the third aisle,
where I had come from

reading the label, to
convey back to her amazing

lure. I was not at all myself.
The sweetness the cookies suggest

had tamed my day,
like lions sitting on barrels.

The circus of it all, ignited
by her name.

TO WRING A SWEETER NECTAR FROM MY HEART IN A FOREIGN COUNTRY

Patrol men follow me in the street,
pura vida in their minds.

Your inebriated self is safe here,
they're telling me.

Why, do I broadcast such love? Did
the New York Times willed again

our wherein virtues?
I'm just off to see one of your natives.

You can slice me
and see a gleam of citrus burst.

No need to follow;
I'm without an army tonight.

MACCHIATO FOR BLACKS

Sippers we see fit in their kept world.
They've eased in their corners, in their minds,
their personal spaces. Active as they were before,
but mellowed, like that of a slowed bee. They've
befriended the hand that fluffs their asters.
It's a politic arrangement but more of harmony.

Sippers we see clinging to their souls.
There is no frail in the comfort we spread
for them. It's all real. Even air has obtained sweet
consistency. And whenever they hear, it is
the tune of forlorn songs. The melody braids
with the lounge-in, the earnest brows. The ones
that linger, well, they, too.

Sippers sit still, wait for the entanglement
of business, so they could buttonhole
the fabric of the day. They can tarry, not sip,
at that same corner, same wide eye; and if it so
happens they feel pang, they go into another space,
release. But this is when relax ends for them.

A MANAGEABLE WAR

Are we to believe that there is one?
A soldier takes a break to peel
a dragon fruit, then resolved
to take a vacation in the jungle.
Some may say this is desertion,
but the colors of the fruit
lures him to taste
what is different.

In Laos, smiling women bring
flowers in their home to brighten
what they see as dark. If
they happen to cross the soldier,
he would calm their fright
and say his bullets are not for them, pleads
with them that they, women,
are in fact sacred. Even to his haggard
foreign self.

They offer him a shower
with the water shimmered from their stove.
On the other burner, they cook
a hearty meal for his hunger. In the
remaining time, he trips over
a bamboo ledge on the floor and
finds what has been missing in his life.
He falls for one of the women and is elated
by her charm and custom.

So much like the dragon fruit, he allows
himself. Then, in the finality,

years after, bearing joy, offspring and all,
he slips back into the jungle, manages
what was not an abandonment
and embraces what
was and is war.

STEP BACK IN "IF TRUTH"

If truth wasn't buck naked all the lies I've kept
out of my pocket would get back in and would
ball an insurmountable amount of lint if truth
wasn't buck naked my belt would also slip out
and leave my pants to harbor another kind of grip
if truth wasn't buck naked my grandmother
would rise again and cook that *miswa* soup she had
claimed would make me a better adult if truth
wasn't buck naked the Dodge truck I'd hoist her in
to attend Mass would bump her higher in the seat
if truth wasn't that buck naked my fourth-grade
teacher would have dubbed me a liar instead of
placing me in that exclusive bubble in which teachers
see creative potential in pupils if truth wasn't buck
naked I would have rotted outside that bubble with
all the diseases known to man if truth wasn't buck
naked the first girl I ever got close to would
have been calmed if truth wasn't buck naked
the tux I had rented would have not clashed with
our consanguinity if truth wasn't buck naked
I would have understood her abrupt goodnight; or
was it mine? If her truth wasn't buck naked chances
are she would have been my wife after ten years
if truth wasn't buck naked truth would have
been grafted on my skin if truth wasn't buck naked
people would likely see pigment in what I see as
clear if truth wasn't buck naked I would stay dry
each time it would storm if truth wasn't buck
naked I would get inside anyway and seek more
of my parents' misguidance if truth wasn't buck naked
my power to predict and turn over a new leaf at
the last minute would seize if truth wasn't buck

naked there would be an end to my allergies my sneezes
would seize like a *rara avis* if truth wasn't buck naked
I'd get a better grip of reality that I am an exhaustion
driven by two uneven legs; or an ear missing
but in favor of that exhaustion if truth wasn't so
buck naked, I would be clothed, but on my t-shirt
there is no pocket of recollection or yen if truth

HERITAGE

Filipino is my footprint, Filipino I will be.
The mold where I came from glistens still in me.
Take part in my shine and I will warm you whole.
Friendliness infects, it burns like coal.
See it on my grin hardening upon your sneer.
It would not crumble, it would not fear.
Basic of needs lift it to wise, free from fall.

Filipino is my heart, Filipino is my crave,
The one I seek in the dark, the light and the grave.
I am a child beyond maturity,
Disciplined in this simplicity I embrace such security.
That woman plays among the stars,
She shifts in their glow, lures in their scarce.
I draw deep from her, she, a well of purity.

Filipino is my rumble, Filipino is my dust,
Spun the wicked tires, wheels christened of rust.
Look into the chrome and be blind of that risk.
I jet from her, the one I love, devoted she resists.
Do not part from her sphere, her attitude, her art.
Our evolution draws that soaked incongruent chart.
Amass me, open me, plant me with that kiss.

Filipino is my nature. Filipino I will be.

AUSTERE

A mother tells her child of the highest,
in adult lingo, that her future is bleak
if she won't take up what is to bear.

Sweet Jesus, thy know small
in that child

How heavy is that to take in
when the girl is still in amazement
of her booster seat?

Sweet Jesus, thy know small
in that child

The Barbies she would go through,
the swag inserted in them, then worrying if Ken
could ever be a play disciple.

Sweet Jesus, thy know small
in that child

Plastic is her first love. The flesh of men
only comes after the bicycle.

DETAINED IN JUNIOR HIGH

See the caged apology,
a young man stuck in his messy room.

He has hung his degree already
at his posh apartment. But

the voice of his mother long gone
is at the rim of his ear

still. Clean this up! But he knows
it has nothing to do

with socks on the lampshade, that the key
dropped is ways from the iron bars,

his hand, arm, stretching close
to the carpet—now hardwood.

Skin near bone,
determined. Aww.

To erase rambunctious.
Frames of girls

are hung crooked,
itching balance.

BACKYARD

Ode to the missing Delphi girls

Down the hill is that hope elsewhere; it doesn't roll here.
We put out humming bird feeders here, which we bought
from an old-name hardware store one of the girls
might have applied in, to have pass-the-time employment.
They were keen to exploring the woods they had grown with.
A father or a brother might have been into hunting,
that they'd wear camouflage wherever, and
the girls would think, "what in the world." To have kin
so out of their touch, so not them. Unlike the bridge
of train tracks, terse beyond this blanket of downcast.
Girls of upbeat could balance on such a thrill
the local "with it" crowd doesn't have to know. That's if
it was the girls' fix being there. Their going away
erases the slate; they're coming back, that's just bone-wet.
They've outworn what is there to outlive, their future
likely to dim our own graces of missed opportunity.
And that down the hill, that's deep rust on the tracks
etched by a hundred storms leading up to this loudness.
No train would bug us further in the night. It's just in us.
No steep slope, no watching themselves climbing down.
We're just prying out every ounce of their souls' breath.

ADJECTIVES AFLOAT

I cross the Rio Grande with my thermos and my lunch.
I'll not stay for long. I'll climb back before I'd drip all my sweat.

There is no lion past the Rio Grande, their beds so lovely
and mythical that they own the charm of sleep, so hush myself

and the wanton mouths I carry. Better grows on that side,
like corn, sautéed in fish. I must be fruitful in years to bury

the papers meant for *compradores de la tienda*, without
the shallow and the threatening. I wade for convenience.

The eagle above has clear sight of heaven, and hell has its
eyes rolling when it sees me at the banks of the Rio Grande.

I'm neither trout or jack rabbit. I am that invisible steadfast,
with reaching baskets of tithe between the pews. We climb that water.

There's no fin on us or hatred for nouns. I swim up either way.
Those rows of green I will dig red. I will plant my ancestors if

they grow still. They're now resting on the Posturepedic,
waiting anxiously to buy me the incandescent Sony.

I will slip by the point of no return. It will own my thirsty,
my hungry, my abetting, my peaceful. My affectionate.

DEFENSE IS A PRIVATE EYE AND A MECHANISM

I'm being watched from a distance,
my clothes suddenly loose on me.
The buttons I've snapped this morning
have rusted to the notion of being
undone. I'm being regarded from far.

The mechanical flow in my head
is speculation, of how could it be.
Time has floated into that stream
I've wakened to, my organic boat
which is porous as yesterday. Yet in

the X-ray of frame, it is that of
solidity. My reflex is to squint, to
redo their stare, their bow down
of what has become idyll in me
I've not surrendered to such,

to look away unworn. My skin is
still tight on me. My skin still
hungers for clarity. It still thirsts
disappearance, as it did yesterday
and the day before.

I'm being watched from a distance.
Be it soulful that doubt owns
every inch of me. Yet every view
from every angle I have to see,
in which I swim in cruel beauty.

MUSCLE LIFE

This morning the flames on Lupine Drive
are all pointing east, to un-divide
more attention. My neighbor

can't seem to harness any of them
as well. He woke pretty early
more sudden than me and saw the colors

ablaze behind his mean-streak Camaro.
I witnessed his liftoff
from my kitchen window, which

is hazed. I have eyes for fire
yet they blink when there's film
smudged from time

gone by, time of no movement. I
empty my coffee; although a step
behind, I hurry to dive into that blaze.

I must shower, still west of my stretch,
west of a fulfilled day.
Once in gear, these flames scorch me

from all directions.

TWO DEER THINKING OF ME

Their eyes pierce through the glass like gestapo, say how dare he
think of us plastic and made in Korea.

We crawl two a.m., but the gall! How could you measure prancing?
This deep in your territory?

We know it's the metro, duh. In your shallow pool thinking capacity,
You don't even know there's a creek

behind that weave fence you look at every morning.
It stretches around your block

while the goddam stream tosses and turns for miles of either way you may think as
the beginning of time.

We don't move a lick. Our patience is your would-be Kodak,
not for you to find your lousy iPhone, but

for our statuesque in this bullet sanctuary we share during the night.
You evolve and gain more brain mulch.

We evolve and get more grace. It ain't rocket science
or you.

AT NATURE DEPOT

At work, it was the wholesale in me
that wanted to know the lake between
me and her, a customer. Hello, I said,
feeling her edges on the shore,
I asked of her footprints, which

I shouldn't have, according
to our guidebook. I should stick
to nice and barter, lend a hand to lift
her heaviest of need, to which I'm
supposed to lend my open mind,

that last notch before "it's yours
for free." But I had a glimpse of her life,
her ever deciduous and green self.
There were currents to smooth,
not in retail. I delved deeper

to throw a stone and skip over
the lovely flow. There, at the bank,
I wanted to mingle with her grace
and sell her nothing. At the day's end,
the sun set on the lake,

pouring out through the "in" door. It drained
into the parking lot, and as I thought
to gather the carts, to see more of her,
my manager halted what was last of my giving
nature and fired me.

ORPHIC SINKS WHILE COLORFUL;
WEIGHTY FLOATS WHILE STRAIGHT

Steady this boat.
Idyllic errors are rocking it

to huh and what.
I stick to the solidity of plain

and boring, to get
me safely back to shore.

Wise, exotic
pencils grate at the moonlight,

heaving prestige, coming
out like a rainbow from lead, but tired,

don't you think?
If you scour the page with subterranean
apostrophes

and Zen-searching
hyphens,

it would be like Woodstock curling
at the beach. What I see out and what you

see in is no longer a pyramid on that sand.
It's burrowing the faculty

in us, which is a dull, camisole-wearing
drag queen with a life vest.

We do see but don't.

NILSPHERE

Things I've bought and not use,
the thrill in them has flown up
to the level I can't reach

or maybe have settled
in the hills and valleys of
a poignant TV show,

a western I used to watch.
Audra and Heath owned
those things now:

an egg timer that can go
more than three minutes, but
not long enough for naps,

an umbrella that
retracts itself to a stool
at a park or anywhere,

a ream of neon paper,
just not 8.5 by 11
to fit the printer.

These things grow old
and disappear
in ambiguity.

But one evening while
I was watching The Voice,
I cited

that one particular singer
who fell from stage and
never sang again.

She might have flown up
and balanced herself
on the stool.

She could rearrange whatever
the chair was among,
idiotic stars?

She might even make the umbrella chair
find its sole purpose and
get my money's worth.

Then that chair would
fall back to earth,
live with me.

SINGLE OUTSIDE

Lamentation is the rolling wheels of trash I hear on Friday mornings
when the bubbles of hot oil try to escape my veins like they're tendering

dove feathers in a steady, gradual count. Kill the soaked peace,
we are under for a reason, not to be dispersed into that wind. Not yet.

It's been 18 years, and the orange suited men think it's time to make
a holiday out of it, so they can recycle the scattered

souls and memory further into bits of misaligned ducks in a row. Shortness
can chafe those who are unfamiliar of tar-raked lungs. To those who

didn't smoke, it had shoved Christ back behind the stone, the stench
circulating among the cave dwellers of the diminishing, of the bargain

hunters and the change hustlers, of the bored and the stretched
handshakers; of good and evil (as long as there is borderline).

Now their kids pop their little capsules of gunpowder out my front door.
You hear it, the anti-*it's just a shot away*. Or is it their parents'? The

millisecond thinness skimmed by powder TV's and uniforms not worn right.
They speak loud when frocks flounce, like Disney had dyed

the moat in a more convincing color: Lavender. Yes, how sweet are the
crocs now. A thought sideswipes my thickness skull. I should go

out, thank those kids (or their parents), and say that they're singled out
still. Of a thousand breathers in these cul-de-sacs, I am betrothed inside.

I have that expanding metal plate to congratulate. But she, who fell, needs
not boil. She can shimmer distantly, in vow and peace, unshy of longing.

ON EACH WILLOW PERCHES KATIE COURIC

Lambswool seemed to drape over her cheeks
that morning. I saw her as my ray of light
each 7 A.M, each normal day.

I didn't lean anywhere then, straight tree over a
pond.
Sky above had never owned metal before.
They were just white streaks, their wheels
tucked in.

The balance in me
or from me was then tipped in the echoes
of her query voice.

Postponed quivering in the branches.
The wind and Katie's thought were at a still,

then they swayed me,
bent me scarred.

DIFFERENCE OF THRILL AND MEMORY

It is your weakness to solve everything in front
of you,
to taste what has not been under your palate,

to breathe the spent air, like in a photo.
May it be black and white, and still the freshness

swoons heavy upon your chest, accustomed
to the uncurled pages your life has not

skimmed through. You call it weakness
because longing bobs from the stern of a boat

unable to reverse.
There is that heave in you to unsnap,

to undo, to have not gone.
Why if the photos are brown from the days

of your ancestors? Would you gasp fresher still,
skip that moment meant to dissolve or be left

behind? Or do you colorize the undrowned,
frightful images that hold your head above?

ATHENS

I've mapped you in my eyes,
deep blue tracing you
in my anxious head. Let me
dance in your streets then,
fling off humility and sigh
in the aged shadows. I'll ferment
in the sweet wine my wicked
soul has not lipped.
I need grasp by your ancient
arms, be it plied by immortal layers,
contoured softly in the now.
Will I fall softly into that opaque,
and be swept by the Caryatid who
has fallen under her own stone?

I hear there's hunger in your gut
and no roof over your head,
Cry of the day. Sigh from the menagerie
on the hill.

Yet I long to see you still. You
be goddess or mortal,
I am in line for your copper vitals,
your warmth by heart,
and that blue, blue
dissipation to own me.

TWO YOKES

So
I'm moving slower now

So
I'm flying closer to the sun

Still, I tuck you
in my young arms,

the embrace they mimic
of every man's pursue

of Helen. Or Clytemnestra,
her twin from all burden.

She does not puzzle fling. She's more my type

in this
evening of moons.

The rain on her face
I'll wipe gently. Yours

is in my soul, dry from any case.
I'll be at your tender.

The two are
just an egg.

SHAKESPEARE ILLEGAL

Who can they fool from the spotlight
when the yonder has wings motorized
to drown the horizon? Stay on the stage
and shut thy trap. It is like me here doing
Elizabethan when the air is obviously
De Niroan. Go fuck the unclean, my poetic
squeam whips me dumb.

The stage is for Hamlet. He too is a fan
of loneliness or being blackest or that hermitic
urge. Swords are not drawn here. Spotlights
dim to give hardened hearts a chance
to drain. But now, the wading migrant is
Hamlet himself no longer single but
in an office party; the river,

his mother. That dark, sub cloak above
lowers still, bloating in the sky
like a counter-terrestrial moon shedding its
extra,
its morality, upon the swimmers with hands
conjoined at what was their childhood in
the stay-put land. This is where youth rattles its
beans of magic.

This is where we tug them to shore, make
sure that the air they breathe is unfucked
clean, not just for survival but for the vitality
in the vote. Actors bleed on stage
but they don't die. The curtains embalm

their body. And on they gasp and gasp and gasp
at opportunity.

FULL FOUR

Bearded knight strengthens in sound,
sight, defying the cosmic aura upon
the New Yorker; it is we who tap this peace
you've grown to hover upon. The hell
with you who can't see the air gap
below our feet, our sails to launch such ship.
We've worn green pants and bike-handled
our mustaches to seize this foggy day,
on your roof of insanity. Let us make
bedlam out of your trite box, wearing
that slim tie or that thin camisole
inappropriate for this funk of a weather.
Seize this Thursday! Let it be your tongue
that taste the sweet molecules in the air;
radical dust will not embitter you, as
long as you see the rise under our boots.
We are everyday. We are that wind,
that hair, the ghost that visits your ribs.
We are that lonely song, that beat,
that shaker of marbles thrown upon
your city walks. We are your fall, your
get up, your dance, your memory.
We are rooftop, and we are Music,
seeping into the cracks of your mundane
little skulls.

PERMISO DE VIEJO

Good evening, I have come to ask for your daughter's hand.
Her dance has lured me this decade past. I've inked her on paper.

I've not shed her two-step off me. I am here to calm your panic,
here in the desert, where erratic birds are supposed to be in my head,

not yours. Under your clay roof, you'll brush hands with my sincerity
and know my skin is burnable under this sun, yet I'll not feel.

It'll thicken for the honor of her inside. I've known her since
the parch of her dance took to fluidity. Like another find in Pompeii

(the bones of a shop clerk frozen in the act fending off ancient looters),
my infatuation craves with only a hairline crack. Intact it still is.

Its restoration defies self-infliction yet none could fit the glove
more. I value your punctilio like I value my belongings,

when minutes away the world may end. May I sit down? Be reassured
that I've come with a dormant volcano in my backdrop.

I'll place her before any harm, on dustless, cool-to-touch brass,
that would inlay the cornice of our living room. She'll smile

upon it, draw exhilaration to continue that beguiling rhythm
on the floor while her identity settles in me. As for your respect,

I say good evening to--with my thumbs pinching and turning
the brim *de sombrero*, if I comfortably, stylishly wear hats.

RIDIN' FENCES

I don't really fit that title
nor that falling down,
let alone sensitive about it.
I'm careful with the splinters
while up there doing my going
against the grain. It's the natural
hide on me, thick as any reason,
and yes, they please me still.

When there's a bet, I don't
hold my queen out in the open.
She's tuck behind my palm,
thick as it may be--calloused
from too many runaway mares.
There've been many jewels
propped up in their velvet boxes.

Arm's reach, but my elbow
don't quite bend. Song and dance
of that scant usually requires
a stable stance. And I find myself
going still; those magnets
at my heels don't care for friction.
The spurs they have spin to my

liking, my urge to be in the range
with that ever-fresh thin glory,
honing in the residue of youth.
Stubborn...but I'll not get snagged
in that soft melt of barbed wire.
I ain't cattle. I'm a driver of swift hooves,
even if my feet get frostbit in this

silly crush with the world.

Got the decency to wear wool
while Earth revolves, my age with it.
Let it spin till my senses
lose their footing, like glacier,
and slide down on that hill,
the gravity my queen'll mistake
for slowing down, or owning up,
amidst this pleasing unstill.

TRUCKS

The TV person says it's better to purchase a truck
than being in a crowded aisle looking for that toy.

We at the couch bought it. The same ad
with a different type and model ran last year.

We think to ourselves, hmm, buy a $35k truck
instead of getting that crazy hoverboard Billy wanted.

We knew it was a class-act bending of the mind.
Or one that totally erased Billy out of our spree.

New features, new crave for power. Our hearts
can chase a truck like they, too, were on radials.

And things get incarnated along the way.
Thrill wills it to happen. Though we prefer seeing

the demo of tug from the rear of trucks,
their flawless bumpers demagnetizing

our eye when they're going away, leaving us safe.
It's when we see the newly designed front grill

that we step back in our amusement. The weight
of wonder does not cause us to breathe easier.

We are in that weight. Billy's heart is in that weight,
Our upbringing of such pulsation bares

down on the same blow--maybe that from a cul-de-sac
south of France or amidst a laidback German village.

Our rearing of kids is often unseen when we find
ourselves at the driver's seat of a truck. The hood doesn't

let us. The best of new options is that camera
that coddles, pampers, and detects the wobbling of

children, not the one high on the pole, which can
never reach down and pull away quickly their arms.

WARHOLA

I am deep within my mind trying to unbury my father
Or pull him out of the mausoleum wall and ask
To jog his identity for a sec and dye his hair

Platinum. Practicality, the gift he died with, has to
Take a backseat to Campbell soup cans, stacked
Evenly to make a fort that houses this story of being

Shot. Was it Valerie Solanas, who loved the edges
Of women, and who took to heart that nothing could
Penetrate her, who took aim at my cellophane-

Haired father? Only to find out what silenced the beat
Meandering in her skull like a bluebird.
Be a gift or be gifted, her tool is a camera that can

Spin the world eight times and not lose the beauty
Of sepiatone. My place rooted on this earth is
That chamber I load. I aim at void, without a palette of

Oils. The red, the ochre, the blues I swirl with
My manic brush. My father died young. He is at a crypt,
At a height I sometime cannot read his name.

DEEPEST

To grow earnest over a new scuba mask, your yin has to ache for no fog. Just frame the undersea like you're watching an intense soap opera, where the actors keep within their lines, cheering for your clarity. Breathe the way your wife used to is to withstand the balmy heat where she grew up--and in which you found so new on your skin. The beach hut you two stayed in is rubber-sealed. How do the windows become misty when glass panes don't exist? If they did, water from the sandy earth saturated the inside of bamboos. The ones that propped up your union. Then it became *this is where I grew up.* You never panicked, never saw fog, never felt leak. It never snowed, just in the cup of her yang you committed yourself to.

CODA

Spur brought her to zig up
from the beaches of Piraeus
to stretch her song.
The stanza needn't be. For she
had me to mellow the rest
of her days. These long-distance
cliques had to crumble,
like dry sponge cake. I
had a whiff, so close, wafting
in the air. Now gone.
Now gone is
the music; her passport
flaking in some sidewalk,
blowing me stagnant.
I walk a locked Paris
now, retracing her steps.
Drifting on to the silent
cuppings of our new
home. Come in, breeze.
Warmth is laid-over.

LADY OF VIEW

She's only blocks away from my solitude
or I'm blocks away from her crowd
She's a place with rooms, the penthouse
holding the very meaning of her,
the ceiling majestic while I curdle
in the floor. And I long for her.

She is a corner in paradise, with narrow
sidewalks so passers go gently rubbing
each other's hips. I sit across
the street, think of how I could graze a part of her.
She is that mauve building with
the white cornice, so seen I ache for her.

Her body and soul are in there, hidden still.
Her hair covers them ever so frail
and suave, it frightens me. So, its strands of sorrow,
then those walls of waning, then
my view of yearn, then my hope in distance,
as I walk back to my solitude.

MET

qualifies me to unfinish
what is disqualified

to take in
consideration what is
qualified to the cinch idea

of what we've started.
We crown that word "cinch"

since we furnished it
for our gradual

for our long haul where
slow cinches

are hung on the wall
we look at them

at eyelevel
and foresee dust

sudden blows
and our eyes flutter away
the cinches

unexpectedly
liquid wells up

in the disqualification
of the unfinished

we analyze the wall
and think maybe

we could paint
over that cinch

but it's too quick; too over,
this fix; this gradual.

CHARLIE

How red was your coattail that the women had each pinched
a part of it? They couldn't let you trip, like a sausage on a stick.
You were intestine sheer, and they saw divine meat in you
as you slither into that stellar house. Follow Charlie, for
he has a halo singeing his wavy brown hair, down to his core.

And cats and dolls were not amused, Black Panthers rolled
in their beaded leather vests. You were their first vision
of the white devil, our first irony of angel cake gone sour
Rot, Charlie, you've ruined the shape of the esoteric lot,
the mystic of their loyal, flimsy walk down that aisle. Rot.

EXODUS NORTH

Grade on my specs
flail not another notch

but I read of this
movement chafed by

the glittery; their Facebook
swishes me out

like a calf amidst placenta,
and I rather

play a xylophone
than hear their moans

and doomsday
alto

what is sweeter
to new breath?

this edge drop
or the stand alert

of his blonde swoop?
I come out,

wishing to see
a Swiffer clean

to this path of
skim milk and honey,

Go, cries any stretch
of imagination, shred

that democracy! Go, mince it
in my feed cord,

yelps any newborn.

AFFAIR WITH A STRANGER

In the nights we left alone
my passport kindled in gray

the need for it
lacked the fiery colors

they were all dancing
in bed;

these hues.

*

Now wakes this creature.
Her body contours mine
like a glove I have yet to take off.
When she moves, the coldness
stays with me. She keeps the warm.

I am not one
for counting breathes.

*

Flashes, like Aphrodites
and untouchables, don't
mingle in my backyard.
I let them by; goodnight
disperses from their ids.
My earth's not a lantern
guiding them to therapy

or to their parked cars.

*

A waking hour delves up
my ceiling and rearranges
       the white mountains
       and unseen valleys up there.

In the morning, they cluster
together again, clean.
       She gets up from my side, expects
       me to miss the taken warmth.

BOON/GOON

I say this, the vacuum we live in has no holes for even
A potus to lie in flowery frequency, yet he owns our ears
Because he used to sit on a wind-bloated throne, which
Now can be installed as a toilet for the many. No one
Rises above the hedge that is constantly trimmed by
The people, for the people who blogs their souls and
Have no plans to perish from the comforts of their home
Or their olive oil-glazed romaine environment. Green
must sustain them. Green, auspiciously gentle as it may

Sound, must be recycled. I say this, the vacuum we slide
Into the closet sucks no dirt, and we don't empty the bag.
Yet we are to be happy with the housework. All must abide
And sift accordingly, to that belief in the carpet and
The underneath. The underside cannot hold pockets of air
As storage where we have to keep the black spots of
Our leader's celestial heart hidden. He must be good.
All must see that. Those misfortunes overseas are lemon
Drops to him. Can't you see he is the valiant sticker

On every chrome bumper we polish and display out
In the freeway made of brilliant ochre? We have made
That Pledge upon our shiniest coffee table for the world
To see. It is fitted between the sarcastic emcee and he,
Our gold-plated trophy. We mustn't smudge such shine.
Humor is at his tongue late in the night flayed beyond
Satellite spread, upon heavy frequency raining on Baghdad.
We're sure they are in spirit there. Their many dead
have since been diced for them to enjoy our Hollywood.

THE POETS UPTAIRS

They're at the plateau where a god can't even
influence the meanness of language and song.
Upper has that cruel love that magnetizes
master-envy or evokes the cuffs of gravity,
where they are always up. Their vitae only rise
like dough kneaded by wizards for wizards and
the conflicts of smooth-skin wizards. The slick is
there, the smooth rhythm which you can only
imagine is diced properly. But the grace at the
bottom never touches whatever blade you've
endowed your jealousy upon. Their words are
felt as usual, like velvet ruffles harlequins wear.
They're not here to make you keel over, over
pain, over heart, over shrill laugh. Stop, stop,
you're reviving me with your pious

jokes, so what we think when we compliment
tirelessly. We hope coruscation will rub on or
rather rub off from a transfusion any of us
would swoon in. It's the upper-level this wonder
of science, this berth in which we are shaken in
large snowflakes and not at all feel cold. Our
hardship is to sigh at the bottom, to calm and
stay. Still we can interfere in their lives. How
passionate do they get beyond these words? Are
their syntaxes connected to their veins? The
milieu in our breathing is that of continuum. Are
theirs that of interruption? We fall asleep not
knowing. They are noisy on their wood planks.
Our floors down below are parquetry, silent,
silent to the rising of stars.

TONTO JOINS THE AMONG

The people around me are top of the world,
Peak of the mound, land of the free,
So much so that they've created a platform
To share their levelness among themselves.
They are the upstairs people to which
The thin floor reverberates their dance
Thinking their loud music won't disturb
The occupants below; I am below them and
Have pattered my stiff shoes according
To their beat, their rhythm. They listen from
Air-suspended speakers to which there are no
Wires feeding in. It isn't because of suave
Or technology that they hang ever so
Effortless. Yes, they think of me underneath
Them or at the side, looking up from my en-
Strangement, my waking up, that I have
Adored their ancestors on print, black and white,
With their ever-welcome sign. Be free,
Because you are at the cusp of downstairs
To our Beauty, our open hands, our graciousness.
Your hands will praise the air someday
And hoist yourself to be among us, sometime,
Someday when the space in our circle is
Unwatched; some week when we don't
Turn our backs to take notice, some month
When your name, your pretty name,
Doesn't stand loud, stand clear, stand out.

WHAT COAGULATES IN VEGAS

A week after, we are still looking for crust under the gel.
The best we can do is tag a footnote under the word
"crust." It stands diminished to something like this: "Depends on
your anti-something, whether it'd be an ounce or capacity

or the weight of your entire body, it would direct your mind
to rule accordingly. It has nothing to do with your skin
or taste or constricting shadow. These are stationary.
They hardly move. Crust shifts under. Crust shifts

most inappropriate, most damaging. Once crust is done,
it wastes the shifting." To be anti-something—anti-paradise,
anti-hotel, antisocial—and harden upon it, the first thing we do
as a crowd is to try to detect the polymer, the there-it-is,

the there-it-sets-forever. Motive is a soaked ribbon
around the killer's neck, the animated will. A week after,
there moved this blurred focus on the inanimate.
What stayed are the wails of souls, thin, jilted, deafening.

MY DRYER BEEPS

It's Halloween, and it's time to dry my nerves
for the winter. Nothing is sacred when
they're wet of worries. The future
won't stand for it because all analyses
would just cling to my old jeans and jacket.
She has been gone for five, yet the walls
are damp of her still. She is too fresh to take
the form of a ghost; if so, I would be
her backbone, the smoke that solidifies her
and lifts her from fulgent lint. I've thrown
away her ashes, but what sacred palpitation
left in me has always whisked her off
at the side of the trash bin. Was I
lonely for the light that shines through her?
Or do the lumens turn into sound
and wake me in my wide bed? No, not so.
I sleep peacefully into another dawn, rested
And quite dry, into this, this Day of All Souls.

AT THE END OF WINDSOR DRIVE

We blink and there
goes our fort, our
lookout tower, if we
kids were mindful

enough. If it rained
the night, we
wondered if it stayed
up, like our spunk.

It was like that of a
sculptor betting on
time. We used what
was in our reach, the

way a crow caws
from just anywhere.
Yes, we were like
the scavengers of

the moment. We had no
patience, our mother
would tell us. We just
whisk by her at the

kitchen with the hacksaw
and a roll of
duct tape behind our
backs, convinced we

were innovative in
a slow-moving adult

world. We hadn't had
time. If we did, our

crow's feet would
leave no mark on the
gooey clay, and up
above, the function of

our lookout tower
would not catch up
or swallow
that beloved blink.

E.E. AND JOHN

You say you've caught up with Lennon
before he was scattered in the moment outside.

They always call homes apartments
in New York, when they lack commas

and capitalization in the comfort, and they ignite
the next moment you two are in. You don't want it

to pass, but rustic seconds prove to titter on hailed fences.
And you worried if he had penned it.

Oh, god, uncapped god, you say, please,
let him have grace shine upon it! If not, dip

my heart in the puddle; spare my soul for the women
I had felt randomly in the streets of Greenwich.

But this medallion I'd always wear through eternity,
as longs as my poems are wicked, undistasteful,

buenoanarchy & offtheedgeflying! Let me stroll in Central Park
and feed the pink pigeons that would guide me

to his Mosaic, to his flat cluster of gentle stones, the
hope of humankind, the nucleus, my nucleus

of this fragmented gray that sublet the dark
in which the stars cannot drown.

I may be dead before he, but when did the universe
constrict to small; or commas arrive to continue?

HOW TO READ WITHOUT KILLING

You angle your eyes at forty-five degrees;
so, your lashes have some sun but not
the politics of the sun. Blinking is good,
knowing in your gut you have wipers
for the unexpected rain your new friend
(or friends) have let in. You gasp a little.
When they really kick you in the shin,
(to take away your thrill and roll you over
like a log), the weight you've read in between
the lines is just unbearable. Your first
intention is to scratch at their eyes—
because you're falling. Who are these spooks?
You wish you had a gun, to bang them off
your wall! Only ignoring could save you now,

that dark figure one who isn't ally, one who
stays in the light, burning all hours of the night.

Like the screen. Their eyes crave your words.
But how could kill be in the plot? Or preference?
How dare they label you and your heroes?
You begin to digress. Your eyelashes lift you
to *ninety* degrees, and there, there in the blinding
light are your friends—true, and at the scene,
with the sun peering via bullet holes in their bodies.

BLACK PUMAS

I've walked in them since she was free of the room.
She may have bought them for me, I don't recall.
Now they have holes in the front and a flapping
soles in the back. Yet I cannot trash them, put
them to rest. I am like her when I am in them,
a slick rooster who always shimmies the sun
any hour of day. And the night is just as loud.
She is the cart of goods ever since he checked out.
My feet breathe the honesty and the calm in
those Pumas. The white has been daubed of dust
not yet settled. I live in them. Frenzy circulate up
from my feet, felt in my bones, throughout my body.
Damned or not damned, I'm pampered in them,
in lush and thorns. The traction they have is sure but
keen as pinched beads not on string, but metal links
clasping certainty. I predicted her breaths would go on.
I would see her another day, in another break.
Those Pumas took me out of the room, in a getaway
she couldn't possibly have seen. To play with her
mind was hardly a thrill a son had managed his time
away, from a once ardent mother. Yet in the wear and tear,
in those quick shoes, quickness shunned from the room,
then from the empty hall, then from the emptiness.

RELAX

Plates move like lily pads, not like broken pieces
of a clay pot. They're always moving, and nothing
is more wicked than the water underneath.
We ride and lie on a chaise. And when rivers break
out, sentiments of rapid overtake our repose,
the way we worship destruction, unseen in our yen.
Yet, in our outside body, the mojito is at our grasp
maintaining peace on the table. Danger claims the rush

to judgment. which draws our heart to immerse.
Why must we blame ourselves? Hmm. And when
water does not speak for a long time, we worry.
We fear the worst, doubting our comfort zone
on that chaise. Plates reassemble underneath us,
continually, as we meander in the lithosphere,
sweetness can't be closer, more soothing, than
this terra cotta we heave our fresh breaths from.

MY GRANDFATHER ENZO

He had nestled in the highest room
on 60 Benedicto Street. He found unity
there or maybe a sanctuary where *mayas*
fly by the window. Or they would come in
and share the coolness with him, away
from the commotion, to think for once

of his younger days, the still cooler air
at Berkeley where he'd measure the area
of this future room and find it grandeur.
He first met his Spanish *sampaguita*,
at the La Union plaza, where the Mary
was always adorned with the flower.

It's too rich to imagine why he chose
to be higher where the walls seemed damp.
With windows closed, it must have been dim,
away from the many *apos*. Yes, wanton.
But to eliminate flaw and find comfort after?

Now as I look up for my own higher ground,
think less of Lolo Enzo's wins only to prefer
a hermit's life—with one grandchild?
Could that place be more of relief,
sound and brutal, if not with mishap?

I was born reversed, always thinking
the sun would always set on my back, never
getting the full grip that it would arc
over me. My grandfather is just those hills
that would turn pink in front of me,
then crimson, then bestially dark.

MUSTANG CROWD

They wear their shirts inside out
Not enough time to see

Their hairs are caked with scented pomade
Yes, they shower

But the soap is supercharged
Thrown against the curve of the tub

They eat steak
Like you wouldn't believe

The vegetarian ones keep to themselves.

CAREFULNESS IN HUMAN USELESSNESS

My apology to you amidst the sociology of me trying to be near you. It's proximity avoiding extremity that levels the stems and flukes on the shelf behind you. If by chance, my heels swing and invert over my head, those vials won't fall and shatter. It is my intention to be on this unbreakable tatter. The glints on the glass are like from the sun peeping through limbs of hanging climbers off an aerial crag. They're desperate of their thrill in peril. But they prefer reliability, the one in their living room while they're watching National Geographic—or Tom Cruise hanging on the same rock but with all the possibility. My approach is in that vicinity.

My apology to you in terminology of me trying to clasp a part of you. I ask for the Spanish word for earring, and in an un-clannish way you provide. So fitting, this "nice" of giving. Permissions are so of device—and relief! A dam of sticks I couldn't disturb then. I stare at you and see no mischief. I side with no flare. Gems just lead to simple admission and issuance. I felt my pulse rev from such constituent. This is how happiness is, the gaining of that rasp in our voice. Nothing is shaved off the top, nothing elapses, nothing of stop or affluent. I wish to be the dust on that café's floor. My approach is loose and all over like that.

My apology to you in the balance of homology in wanting to stay. Like the table with uneven legs, you see me in need of sturdy while still chanting along unstable. So, you place napkins under each foot to level me out. My thought in revel is that you care for such commotion to quiesce, for absolute peace. Enough to make me feel at home, diluting the distance. The dome over my head I carry, still with scary debate. It is fate, this intention to jog any exclusion. Fences are clear, I know. But they fog up my lenses. This, my approach, to jump over, fight off the fall. It is my egg, to poach, to fry slight, over that nothing at all.

DESTINATA

Here tangled dreams bubble up keen

> like when I rose each morning to make sure
> my electric Royal had plenty of ribbon, when
> that ribbon did not really empty anywhere
> or wasn't near the word "plenty" because it went
> from spool to spool. The black never gets
> smudged, but the red. It harrowed on the blinds
> before my neighbor's window, so close to the side
> of our house that their daughter could hear
> my clacking away—and my breathing when the lights
> were off and hers was on. Caution did not slap me
> on the side of the head. Prurience played me. Itch
> was innocent, in care of what I'd scratch in my future,
> that brisk silence in the good dark, in care of want
> and solitude. Or was that the mother?

And climb the algaed stucco wall.

> But you ached and was sleepless when you heard
> that North Park Plaza had allowed a dance bar
> to nestle in where the record shop used to be,
> right next to Burger Chef. All of your inside
> twisted and turned then, when you saw across
> the bypass that it wasn't a dance club where
> you partake in the dancing. No. What was this?
> Had your midwestern town become exotic
> overnight, where loneliness seethed into gross
> domestic product? Had all this evolved when you
> and your brother tinkered on the Ford Capri,
> muscling it into a fake V-8? What your parents
> had not diagnosed about you, when a trite skin

74

club existed in your brain!

It's not slick or bowed like Byzantine

But you went on to college and study the eroteme
and ellipsis of a decent human being, so
far,

It just pushes you with the sharpest of fall.

And in the third year (four more to go and
decipher?), that ecclesiastic feel of undone willed
you to drink tequila and dark beer, because you
thought you had to attain that prestige, that
equilibrium in manhood.

Shadows stretched long before you. Your father
insisted on deeply planted clues while your mother
merrily watered them. Yes, you said, if you could first
travel the world, somewhere hot, maybe see a different
city each year you were in school!

She came in slowly, her one gentle step.

Ah, Costa Rica, and a girl walking the cobbled road
sequined further by little chuckholes, inches
deep of copper water. You thought she needed a ride
by the way she took her time. But it was her affectation.
The Jeep Compass rental would surely get her faster
to that roadside all-things-needed store. But she was
a nursing student, and her anti-bar, anti-night humility
struck your head so hard it kept your elusive heart
in the glove compartment. She wouldn't hop in
at first—till the rear tire had splashed her whites.

Her lips comelier still, which you first deny.

> And seek not the willful (meet the parents
>> type), the caring
> pretend occupied eyes.
>> Never mind the daring aim of life.
> It's but to cull the dishes
>> free of nerves and of flies!

But her touch stretches your youth inept,

> Dear Professor:
>
>> I am writing to you in confidentiality, ahead of
>> my parents, that there may be a bump on the road
>> that I have travelled over the break. Unfortune is
>> temporary and not necessarily a misfortune.
>
> Dear Student,
>
>> What bump on the road is this? You know I am closer
>> to your mother and father than I am to you. But I'll give
>> you my mute. For now.
>
> Dear Professor:
>
>> Nothing that can't be solved by time or by me getting
>> serious employment once I get back in September.

It slips you unkind through the Bridge of Sigh.

> Legend has it
>> freedom is at one end,
>>> and chain and ball at the other.
>>> But you wanted both

to coincide in the slipping through,
    and the life lesson
        still on the pages of
            Psychology 202, and your
                frame of mind is in the projector
                    lighting up the wall.

For winter has whirled white about your room.

    I distill myself in the place where I had been poured,
    The sound of water clashing on fertile ground, and
    the whisper of seeds splitting, taking my scheme upward.
    I was once dry, now wet. She couldn't bear a child
    without complications, like the murmur of adults
    in the backyard, swilling in the promise of a grandchild,
    that joy of a cookout where I broke the news,
    in the pleasing smoke. I'll be the grass that they'll nourish
    and groom. No need to fold her in over worry or wither.
    Summer will end. And the sound of muscle and that
    of wicked speed down the alley will come to a screech.

Yet at the sill, she's painting midnight;

    it's opaque
    but she prefers
    brighter moods,
    like her own mother upright
    with the original lupus,
by the window.
    Orange,
    gray,
    burnt...
    Not those,
    please. I'm cradling
the back

of her head

In the coming days you feel the restless doom

> for it is strengthening your interest in the interior.
> How could it be visional all of sudden? The fragility
> in mid-air. The dew-beaded web of a spider is
> crested in your thoughts. What should you do now?
> You have her in your hand, yet she's going.

For she darkens helpless any wedge of light.

> She is that orchid your mother mends every morning.
> Two years your mother has kept it anew.
> From far, it's angel hair, a baby son's breath.
> Twenty-four months you must have been a bouncy kid.
> A hundred and four weeks your mother would have spent
> Comparing you and her, sensing your compatible.
> Days with her you didn't measure but lived each one.

For you stay steadfast to origins.

> Where are those? That tone your professor owns in the calm.
> It was just here, around you. Grip from it can't be felt.
> It was grasping you, lulling you, taking in warmth
> that shrouded both of your bodies.

You shiver in the kin binary.

> There is   /   yours un-
> no such   /   evenly matched
> level.   /   her outlook.

She's willing given, her deflating life thus begins

For I stood to continue weighing on this earth
While she is repose yet unleveled from my reach

She strengthens me still without the hope of her
Go on to continue my last four

Then comes beautiful Venice as my escape
her suggestion, a sanctuary to be in

Talons clasp your breath, her soul you must carry.

This has flipped your idea

of corner dance
                    alone
sigh
            of life
when
            it ends

                    you leave Venice,
spiral first

                                        then
                                            turn to the ailing

in Costa Rica,
            mend the mother

                                her

                                continue